Hillary, Made Up

Hillary, Made Up

Marianne Kunkel

STEPHEN F. AUSTIN STATE UNIVERSITY PRESS
NACOGDOCHES, TX

Cover and book design by Sarah Denise Johnson
Cover art and photography by Johnathan Loesch

For my two-year-old, Arlo, who napped while I wrote

Contents

Hillary, Made Up

Eyes

Tweezers to Hillary

I'm like an expert chef who knows when
to walk away and let a stew sit:
I didn't go near your brows in the '60s,
so perfect were the arches

like plump, dark dolphins leaping
out of the water, almost
nuzzling, save for the foam-
white bridge of your nose.

I held back in the '70s, too,
when your wire aviator glasses
slouched down your cheeks, and unlike
others harmed by this style

your thick, chocolate brows stamped
your face with cheerful vigor.
By '92, your coif was champagne
and eyes blueberries

on the verge of bursting, cramped inside
ovals of oily eyeliner, pricked
by mascara-petrified stray lashes,
and still I abstained.

But few see the wisdom of restraint.
Before your move to the White House
a crew cornered you with a bloated bag:
age serum, seaweed peel, tweezers.

Did you hear me scream? How could you
when all they left were skinny brows
with tapered ends like bony fingers
angled out to plug your ears?

White Eyeliner to Hillary

The cocaine of makeup,
I turn an exhausted face
into a hopped-up, hyped-out
who's-ready-to-party
mask. Just ask the stylist
who, after your flight
from L.A. to Brooklyn,
dabbed then smudged me
on the inner corners of your eyes.
At that night's debate
you were brighter than
Bernie's hair, your skin
the highest-watt porch light
on a twinkly street. Come
September, a cough
blazed your lungs, burning
hours off your sleep regimen;
the doctor gave you pills
and said *pneumonia* while
the stylist triple-traced me
along your lower eyelids.
And that's how you arrived
at the 9/11 commemoration,
looking impossibly awake,
your fried, bloodshot eyes
not as noticeable
as my cheery chandelier hue.
It's too bad nobody applied me
to your legs, which buckled,
or your tongue as men
helped you into a van.
To Chelsea's apartment,
you croaked, while back
at the park, friends like me
wanted another swipe at you.

Contact Lens to Hillary

Those who call you private,
distant, and colder than a voter line

in Bismarck in November
should see you now as you gingerly

balance me, a tiny bowl,
on the soft pad of your pointer finger.

You're like the gentlest elevator
as you lift and tilt me to face your large eye

which twitches, yet you don't blink.
Just when I could slip off your finger

you thrust me, a foreign object
as instinctively unwelcome as Russia

poking into your emails,
and I latch onto your cornea,

the most sensitive tissue that bends
the world's light on its way to your brain.

I'm this close to you because today
you'll speak to young women

despite losing the election
mere months ago, a historic blow

that would drive others
into their home, into a shabby bathrobe

and old, crooked bifocals,
keeping even the neighbors at arm's length.

Brow Pencil to Hillary

To all the little girls who are watching this: never doubt how valuable, how powerful, and how deserving of every opportunity you are to pursue your own dreams.
—Hillary Clinton

Have you heard? The new trend's
power brows, making them big

as blackboard erasers, archless,
and furrier than chows. Teen models

sport these caterpillars effortlessly,
too young to have ever plucked

like mad back when the trend
was dental floss-thin brows, back when

a woman could catch tweezer fever
and uproot every last frail hair,

then sharpen me and, like calligraphy,
draw dainty arches. Now I fly off shelves

for a different use: women
with endangered or extinct brows

want power brows, the look
of a feral beast, the exhilarating addition

of fear and awe to a first impression.
Like a protein shake, I bulk up brows,

my tip deliberately blunt
for long, broad strokes that shade in

every woman's barren arches.
Have you noticed your stylist applying me

more thickly lately? Do your fabricated
bushy brows remind you of wild,

unfettered childhood? Just think, girls
today preserve each strand of power,

aware their mothers chase substitutes,
aware strong brows are only the beginning.

Brow Brush to Hillary

Your world's a surplus of old, scruffy men—
furry-eared judges, diplomats whose teeth
match buttered popcorn, senators who spend
more on cigars than anti-aging cream.

Don't get me started on their eyebrow nests.
Hairs sprout north, south, east, west, as if neglect's
in vogue, as if the longest, wiry pests
wave at their brothers—stubbly chin and neck.

Meanwhile, I rake your clipped brows into place,
frequently pausing so stylists can pluck
a few distracting hairs, or fill bald space
they over-plucked. The next unshaven shmuck
who wishes you good luck before a speech
will see me bristle—luck is men's private beach.

Eyeliner to Hillary

If she gets to pick her judges, nothing you can do, folks. Although the Second Amendment, people, maybe there is.
—Donald Trump

You spy me in your stylist's hand
and huff *Here comes the lasso*
and for once, I'm not bothered;
I ring your eyes cinnamon brown
as your plane's many TVs
replay the orange-skinned man's
death threats. Your staff is still.
One adviser tries to sleep
while others scroll tweets,
hoping for mass public outrage
about the suggestion to shoot you.
You alone act normal: fidgety
while I skate your eyelids,
shaking your head when your stylist
proposes a smoky double-line effect.
I've prettied more patient women
but 36,000 feet above ground
their crimson smiles fade away;
how can people want to kill you?
Once I imagined drawing a tall fence
around your body to block out staff,
phones and binders, forcing you to see
my elegance, but I've never wished
for a bullet to pierce and destroy you.
I seal an *O* at your eye's edge
and picture your skittering bright-blues
shut and stitched over with black *X*s,
that thread of old meant to prevent
the dead's eyes from opening.
Are any of us really surprised?
you suddenly turn and ask
your staff, tearing the barber's cape

from your neck and waving off
your stylist. Staff jolt in their seats
and you start planning a counter-move.
Before I'm zipped inside a dark bag
I hear the pilot announce a storm;
I'm still thinking of *X*s and *O*s
and if I could, I'd tell you how sorry
I am hatred has stolen your safety.
I'd ask the rain to wash away
this war like it does a chalky tic-tac-toe.

Eyelash Curler to Hillary

If only you could capture voters' hearts
as easily as I grab lashes, clamp
them in my silver jaws, and turn stray parts
into a whole. Those in the far-right camp
hate you beyond repair, like bubble gum
in hair. Those in the middle wouldn't dare
be feminists; they're why I left Lancôme
and live beside your campaign makeup chair.
Most harmful, Bernie's fans echo his slur—
establishment—like some say I'm too mired
in history compared to all-plastic curlers.
Vogue calls my steel design clunky and tired
but I work best for squeezing lashes hard.
Our biggest sin is doing well so far.

Mascara To Hillary

You don't realize how good
    you have it. To turn the heads
        of Egyptian bachelors

in 4000 BC, women mashed
    dried crocodile poop
        with kohl and honey, a vile paste

into which they dipped Q Tip-shaped bones,
    then coated their lashes
        with one hand, the other

pinching their nose. In ancient Rome
    women burned fruit pits and flower petals
        then squeezed plump elderberries

over the ashes, determined despite
    juice-stained fingers
        and smoke-steeped hair

to paint sludge on their lashes.
    You don't appreciate how safe
        I am now, not like in 1933

when a man invented
    eyelash dye—coal tar sold in tubes
        with little brushes; when a woman

in a hospital wailed that her eyes
    were bonfires, it was too late,
        her corneas

settling into blindness.
    I could be newly waterproof,
        its first recipe half-turpentine

so swimming pools reeked
      of pine and women in them rubbed red,
          itchy eyes. Lucky you

to be around in 2016
      with my curvy, self-coating wand,
          my tube with a silver ring on top

for scraping off excess liquid—
      a perfect mixture of pigment,
          wax and tiny fibers for thickening

your lashes. Yet minutes before a debate
      you bat me away
          to review your notes. Mr. Trump

and his entourage saunter
      down the hall and you glimpse
          his plain face, his untouched

pockmarks, his spider-veined cheeks.
      Masked by his whistle, you whisper to a stylist
      Does he know how good he has it?

Brow Gel To Hillary

7.5% of patents granted are granted to women.
—National Bureau of Economic Research

Chances are my inventor is male,
someone who squeezed cheap hair gel
into an ex's old mascara tube
that had rolled behind his toilet.
I imagine him jiggling the bristly wand
into the tube, remembering his ex
licking her fingers and smoothing her brows.
When I debuted on a store's
bottom shelf, a tube of colorless gel
even stylists deem low-priority,
I saw a man with slicked-back hair
hang his head, sigh and trudge away.
Your stylist took a chance on me,
only for you to look me over
and ask *Is that necessary?* Though I tried
to hate you, long after we met I dream
of your flashy colors: chartreuse pantsuit,
gold chunky necklace, hair
like a yellow highlighter, and lipstick
as richly red as any I saw in a store.
I'd trade my invisible, trivial life
for a second as your midnight mascara
or coral blush. I think of you today
as your stylist, whom you let go,
chats with a client about a recent march
and the millions who knitted pink,
cat-eared hats. She says you didn't march
and I'm shocked picturing you hatless,
colorless, but surely, like me, you admire
those fired-up women flooding streets
donning bright pink inventions.

24

Eye Shadow to Hillary

In the bag where I live, I brag
to new makeup that I used to touch
your eyelids, painting them taupe with an arc

of pearly peach just below each eyebrow.
I describe the day I met you, when my owner,
your stylist, opened my rectangular lid

to reveal all twenty-four shades
and you pointed to my lightest corner
and said *Those colors look good.*

Powders and creams *Ooh* at your compliment.
I never tell them you said *Nothing garish.*
You may have thought my violet or burnt orange

was too risky for someone running for president,
or heard bold colors on pale eyelids
look too clownish;

the truth is, more than you
wearing the same corner of me every day,
I'm most proud of one Friday morning

at a black women's symposium
when you shared a makeup room
with two other speakers.

Your stylist finished your face
an hour early, turned to the women
and said *I'm a big fan. Can I do your makeup?*

Then she skidded her brush across my emerald,
cerulean, tangerine and fuchsia,
tickling parts of me for the first time,

robust shades that mellowed to a soft glow,
contrasting beautifully against their dark skin.
When the crowd began chanting

your name, the makeup room emptied.
I never learned the black women's names.
I dream of a day my owner works

for a presidential hopeful who's not white
and more of my shades are dipped into,
her eyelids ushering in a rainbow.

False Eyelashes to Hillary

*I don't ask for a life of luxury, the world's gold or its fine pearls. I
ask for a happy heart, an honest heart.*
—"Calon Lân"

Days after losing, you appear on TV
wearing brown mascara, blush
and muted lipstick, yet viewers swear
they can't see an ounce
of makeup. *Must be too glum
to line her lips,* they say.
*Why bother with mascara
when she knows she'll cry?*

That night, you scrub the color off your face.
I watch from my small plastic case
where I wait, with nine others like me,
for you to glue me to your eyelid, pinch me in place.

I'm starting to think I'm the only makeup
you've truly quit. I'm the kind
not meant to make lovely features lovelier,
but to replace all women's lashes
with little uniform brooms.
I remind you that sometimes fake is better.

Viewers don't get to see your towel-blotted face,
your puffed cheeks as you swish mouthwash,
or hear your gentle hum
of an old Welsh song
so pretty, so undecorated.

Skin

Foundation to Hillary

Maybe a real person doesn't exist underneath there.
—Jon Stewart

Your fans would love to know you as I do:
each morning, save for Bill's occasional kiss,
I touch you first. Before fake lashes, glue,
dark liner on your brows, eyelids, and lips,
plum blush, concealer, balm and blemish cream,
your stylist lightly dabs me on your chin.
Gauze-thin, I skim your cheeks and leave beige wings,
then graze your nose and forehead, closing in.
Some people want to kill you: *Lock her up!*
they shout, and worse. Some people gruffly shrug
when asked your ideology. Makeup
is layered goop and powder, piled like rugs;
I'm sheer so other products have room, too.
If Americans could ease off, they'd reach you.

Powder to Hillary

They don't call me compact for nothing.
When snapped shut, I'm an airless sandwich,

my flat, pink puff the baloney
between mirror and talcum cake.

I'd trade my cramped quarters
for your hurried legs and swinging arms

though I don't envy your tongue
which, like my puff, only flies

with others' guidance. During this campaign,
beside a stylist patting my dust

on your face are always advisers
buzzing about *likeability, authenticity*

but never anger, and a *glass ceiling*
that sounds like my clear, plastic lid.

Is your ceiling also claustrophobically close?
With the right pressure

you'd think they'd crack, but it's more likely
I'll be trashed when my cake runs out,

not for a splintered lid.
Landfills are full of my kind,

basins hollowed and puffs dingy
yet lids unscratched. Here's my advice:

treat your ceiling as if it's made of steel
so your whacks are twice as hard.

Woo every male voter you can,
but don't forget to charm

the other gender. After all, it's women
who throw me out without a second thought.

Lip Plumper to Hillary

young women in this hall feel the Bern
you hear their high-pitched chants

from backstage as a stylist dabs me
on your lips and my menthol and cinnamon oil

tingle and burn until your lips swell
making you look younger than you are

your lips have thinned over time
and voters say your age is a liability

minutes from now you'll debate Bernie
and the young women who say sexism is over

will see their future in him not you

Face Primer To Hillary

*...what was perceived as her membership in the dominant class, all
cleaned up and normalized, aligned with establishment power rather
than the forces of the resistance, and stylistically coded...*
—Susan Bordo, *The Destruction of Hillary Clinton*

Anyone who's painted over an already-
painted room, turning burgundy walls
yellow or beige walls bright green, knows
to first apply primer, a substance stickier than paint

that grabs hold and glazes walls
impenetrably white so crayon and mold stains
disappear, so decades-old black paint
can't bleed through. I work the same way,

ivory-hued, gooey makeup that tinges your lips,
cheeks and lids a color purer than bare skin;
I block out complexities in your complexion
and make every cool blue vein vanish.

On this blank canvas, a makeup crew confidently
adds red lipstick, coral blush and eye shadow
and mahogany eyeliner; each product shines as if electric
against your uncomplicated skin. But what no

paint or makeup salesperson will admit is primer
sometimes works too well. Seeing you now,
when I've erased your natural face
and replaced it with one-size-fits-all glamour,

some voters forget your humble beginnings
interviewing migrant workers to better
their health and education, going undercover
in desegregated schools to fight discrimination,

visiting families with only a smile
plastered on your face. A homeowner feels your pain
when she primes and paints a room, tan to teal,
then a friend asks *Wasn't it always this color?*

Retexturizing Cream to Hillary

What I wanted to do was soften and feminize her look and make her someone women can totally relate to.
—Kriss Soterion, makeup artist

When Kriss brought me to you, she'd just
mixed me up in her car, an impromptu blend
of oil, water and dye with a little acid
stirred in for burning off dried-up skin cells.
Like twins, we were born seconds apart—
me, a new cream, and you, radiant.

Kriss smeared me on creases around your eyes,
above the bridge of your nose
and beside the corners of your mouth
called *crow's feet* and *marionette lines*,
cute names for hated wrinkles. *This'll sting*,
she said. You asked if she meant me or aging.

When you took the stage that night in '07,
my light-reflective properties made you glow
with a youth that rivaled Obama's,
a calm that outdid Edwards', a shine brighter
than Biden's frosty comb-over. Emails
poured in to Kriss asking how she did it.

Others didn't ask, assuming Botox
or plastic surgery. Soon speculation soared
to dangerous heights; women voters
Kriss wanted to like you saw in your taut face
their shortcomings, as familiar
as air, as habitual as cosmetic chemistry.

Nail Polish to Hillary

Paparazzi think you and I
are strangers; they've snapped
bags under your eyes,
white scrunchies in your hair,
and pantsuits in every color, but never
your ordinary-looking fingers as you
shake hands with voter after voter
after voter. Not flashy
or loud like their cameras,
I'm clear and low-gloss.

One badgers *Will you beat Trump?*
as you near your campaign van
and you meet his eyes and shrug,
an honest answer, but it won't stop
doctored photos of you
beside the headlines *Liar* and *Crooked.*
You heave the van door open,
fingers showing, but nobody zooms in
for a shot of me, of us,
the headline *Transparent.*

Concealer to Hillary

I blot out your every blemish,
        pimples, blackheads, whiteheads,
                craters acne left behind;

my tube of goop and spongy wand
        hide warts, sties, a benign mole
                on your right cheek,

chickenpox scars from 1953,
        an eyebrow scar a year later
                from tumbling off your bike;

I camouflage faint freckles,
        a tiny bell-shaped birthmark on your chin,
                under-eye circles on days

your campaign schedule
        bloats with back-to-back rallies and interviews;
                I coat you in safe and less safe chemicals

covering wrinkles, age spots, spider veins
        branching your nose and temples,
                smile lines and frown lines;

then I laugh at all the voters, many
        who wear me too, who swear
                you're definitely lying about something.

Lipstick to Hillary

Your makeup crew convinces you to keep me
in your pantsuit pocket. I fade fast, and a touch-up
after a long speech and some hasty sips of water
turns your lips raspberry red again. You joke my tint
is called Reassuring Red because a poll of likely voters
prefers me to your real lip color—mottled beige.
I've felt your teeth, crowned, wide, while en route
to Coral Springs to meet the mayor; our car
swerved and your rushed hand slipped, sending me skiing
through your half-open half-pout—how every woman puckers
her mouth for me. Sometimes I'm proud we're close,
when floods of fingers flutter over guardrails
just to graze you. Sometimes I cry for a different owner,
a shy freshman to delicately glide me along her lips,
blot me, gloss me, trust me to hook the heart
of her horny lab partner. *If only it were a cigarette,*
you joke to your makeup crew then drop me
in your pocket; the debate begins and Mr. Trump
waves his arms, describing a border wall.
You carefully scrawl small words, your black pen
thin and beveled like me, yet you hold it much longer—
it's a rose and your hand's a vase, snug, graceful.
When you say your opponent hides crimes in his tax returns
he shouts *Wrong wrong* until you pause and seal your lips,
no longer raspberry red but ashen apple. You don't
wear the kiss-me face of a string bikini model
but as he keeps interjecting, you don't look rattled either.
This, finally, I understand: only I know when I'm on
my last twist, one sunny coat away from empty,
just like you never show when your patience is thinning.

Blush to Hillary

The application of artificial blush may mimic this vascularization,
providing a subtle signal of sexual interest or arousal.
      —Theresa E. DiDonato, *Psychology Today*

Psychologists lie. I couldn't care less
if I make someone want to pop your blouse,
kiss your stomach and wet
your garden of pleasure until your cheeks
bloom roses. Sounds boring to me.
My mind's out of the gutter
and in offices, restaurants, truck stops—
everywhere a woman works for less money
than a man yet still squeaks apologies
when he interrupts her, demands
she smile more, or confuses her maternity leave
for no dreams of promotion.
I'm the outrage women can't show,
a simulated ruby stain standing in
for a stamped-out flame. I gave my all
at your town hall debate as Mr. Trump,
bully driver, stood eerily close behind you,
his noisy breaths noxious fumes;
while your eyes steadied on voters in front of you
I glowed siren red. Now you're out
of work, twiddling thumbs
for Russia's amusement. I'm not surprised
you wear me less. Enough simmering anger—
flip your burners to high.

Setting Spray to Hillary

I was the letter Z, caboose, your last
cosmetic. After an hour of oils, creams,
wax pencils and powders, your stylist asked
you to close your eyes and mouth and count to three—
mascara not yet smudged by power naps,
blush bold but not too bold, mauve lips still bright,
she spritzed me ear to ear. Your makeup, trapped,
looked fresh as polished fruit all day and night.
Given that I pause time, how could I see
an end to us? Early November 9th,
your stylist caked your face with all but me,
sloped on a shelf. Your odd purple attire,
Bill's frown, your words *This loss hurts*—I deduced
your round-the-clock finesse had no more use.

Lip Gloss to Hillary

I'm sorry that we did not win this election for the values we share and the vision we hold for our country.
—Hillary Clinton, concession speech

Who knows why you decided, of all words,
to say *sorry*? History didn't force

you to; men in your place, looking tired, hurt,
groaned *I regret* and *The failure's mine, not yours*

but never *sorry*—a word women drop
less if they've goofed than if they want to seem

non-threatening and soft. Like soda pop,
was *sorry* sweet refreshment to redeem

your image after such a heated race?
Or did you see what fans saw—a new world

where science, immigrants, health, a broad tax base
are gone—and took the blame like a good girl?

I can't help thinking I was there as grease
to loosen your pursed lips, let *sorry* leak.

Bronzer to Hillary

The sting of losing has worn off.
In its place is manageable sadness,
      sniffles in the shower,

and an occasional laugh
about absurdities
      of your campaign—

this morning over breakfast you tell Bill
Look what I found
      while waving me,

a plastic case containing a disc
of light brown powder
      and a hinged mirror.

I've lived in a basket of towels
in your bathroom
      for months, tumbling there after

a campaign stylist
turned over her bag on your counter
      while searching for a tiny brush.

You shake your head at me and chuckle.
She used to dab this
      on my face so I'd look tan

and Bill cocks
an eyebrow, not understanding
      what's funny. More chuckles—

Voters never asked
how I found time for the beach.
      Bill studies your face, a mix

of amusement and disbelief
at the lengths
       you went to win.

He slaps the table, rises
and says *Let's drive*
       to Lake Welch Beach

and later as he packs
the car, you slide me
       into a padded envelope

on which you've scribbled
the stylist's address. Then we make
       our necessary journeys, mine home

and yours to a surging tide
as out of your control
       as grief.

Blotting Paper to Hillary

The weirdest thing about me is that I don't sweat.
—Hillary Clinton

I chuckle when an intern stashes me
in your emergency cosmetics bag;
it's June in Raleigh, 92 degrees,
no shade on stage, no breeze rippling flags,
and you alone resemble crisp, clean sheets.
As you shout *More good jobs!* I long to dive
into the crowd and sop up oily cheeks,
damp noses, sandaled feet, babies' greasy thighs.
You shout *I believe in science!* and describe
fast-melting glaciers, angry seas, whole towns
submerged by 2030; would a tribe
of blotting papers help? We could tamp down
high, grimy waters and mop the frenzied brows
of all the politicians laughing now.

Chapstick to Hillary

That is going to take an individual that has testicular fortitude.
—Paul Gibson endorsing Hillary Clinton

My home's a makeup bag,
      but I can roam as others can't

since I'm genderless; male presidents
      and senators get dry lips, too.

You've popped me open in Sacramento,
      Montpelier, Austin, and Little Rock.

I've slicked your lips as often as I've seen silos,
      structures like me

on steroids. There was a day I slipped
      from your palm onto a sidewalk

and met ants who couldn't budge me.
      I was their king. There was the day

you visited a rural clinic and watched
      a pap smear;

from your pocket I glimpsed pink flesh
      glossy like my wax, my heart, my core.

Lip Liner to Hillary

I'm worried sick you'll ditch me. Rumor is
Sarah Palin's lips always look plump
because her liner's tattooed, counterfeit.
She wakes up with zigzag hair, bad breath, a grump,
and fuchsia-outlined lips ready for prom.
I hear her trick saved time at campaign stops;
unlike your fifteen-minute drill—lip balm,
lip primer, me, lipstick, gloss, cotton swabs
to even my line—she was done in five
and flashing a calm smile beside McCain.
But hear my case for keeping me alive—
you shower and my dye slinks down the drain
along with peach powder, mascara wax;
bare-faced, you know what's you and what's a mask.

Makeup Remover Wipe to Hillary

You know my sister,
        the baby wipe, from precious years cleaning
your baby daughter's pink bottom;
                one sniff of a lavender-scented wipe
        is enough to remind a woman of young motherhood,
early hours shushing a fussy infant
        as the sun also squirmed, rising and pouring light
into the nursery. You've used my other sister,
                the disinfecting wipe, to sanitize your peanut-dusted,
        wineglass-ringed coffee table after
guests headed home;

                        you and I go back
to your first run for president, when a friend
                gave you fifty of me in a pocket-size pouch
and said *Here's a convenient way to wash*
        your face. That night, you climbed into bed,
                reached for me and felt the same cool dampness,
the same slight furriness of my woven fibers, as women all across America;
                no matter how fancy or cheap their makeup,
no matter their race or age, they drowsily wipe their colorful faces.

Male politicians say they understand women
        as well as you do, as if empathy's easy as knotting a tie,
but do they ever glide me or my sisters along a surface?
        What you realize, like millions of women,
        is that sometimes the biggest messes require
the simplest clean-ups, a little patience and elbow grease;
        you'd lead by ridding the country of war, hunger, disease
        one spot at a time.

Hair

Headband to Hillary

If Clinton wins, headstrong [sic] bands will be the next first lady fashion trend.
          —USA Today

It would've been easy to let me go.
Bill announced his run for president
and mere hours later, friends rang
your doorbell, heads obscured
by puffy garment bags. Gliding
inside, they snatched my simple arch
from your hair and flung me
in your bedroom's trash can; the lid shut
as pearls snapped on your ears,
or was that snap a belt cinching
a cashmere skirt around your waist?
I didn't see you until late
that night; the lid popped open and more
extraordinary than Bill's shrill snore
was your bright smile, wide as me.
You draped me on your dresser
and, the next morning, returned me
to your head, my casual embrace
preventing stray hairs as you
dined with donors and waved
with Bill at rallies. It would've been easy
to toss your independence in the trash
beside me. Yet we live on.

Hair Curlers to Hillary

you may not remember us
but we sure as hell
remember you

we were hot as blacktop in July
waiting on a stylist to lacquer you
the First Lady

with lipstick
and slather lavender eye shadow
up to your eyebrows

we blared our tinny alarm
to say our temperature was Sahara-high
we were ready for action

but not until a man
beside a camera yelled
Fifteen minutes!

did your stylist reach for us
she rolled long limp strands of hair
around one of us

then another
then all ten
stopping just before your scalp

and fastening us in place
with our matching
hot pink plastic clips

we blazed like happy logs
in a flameless inferno
never expecting you to scream *OUCH!*

and point to your forehead—
one of us tucked in your bangs
had drooped and singed your skin

and as your stylist
swooped in
you fought fire with fire

demanding
she remove us all
then the man by the camera floated over

and in a low voice said
Americans only listen
to glamorous women

later in the White House library
cameras rolling
your hair was perfectly curled

into big hair-sprayed arches
and you described to the public
a new health care plan

that made enough people
boiling mad
it soon failed

you can't say you weren't warned—
even greater than your power
is the power in numbers

Hair Spray To Hillary

Everybody likes a camera, a magic box
that stills crashing waves, freezes a child's flip on a trampoline
and captures a periwinkle sunset;

and most everyone likes museums,
high-ceilinged halls lined with elaborate dinosaur skeletons,
permanently-fanned butterfly wings,

ancient mummies, weathered buffalo drums
and gilded portraits of queens, even ones still alive, so attached are we
to staring hard at things meant to move;

and many women (and some men)
like me, defier of nature, turning the most bendable texture
into a fragrant statue,

stiffening ringlets, loose curls, finger waves,
french braids, chignon buns, fades, Afro puffs, mohawks, bangs
and for you, a presidential feathered bob;

but less than half of Americans
like you, whom many accuse of behaving robotically—
stilted speech, plastered smile—

as if they're surprised you present
your best, as if they haven't made you a cheerful, careful woman
stuck grinning as you contemplate this spinning Earth.

Wig to Hillary

She has a new hairdo… Is that a wig?
    —Donald Trump

When you let Jimmy Fallon tug your hair,
the world saw it was real. Though I believe
you, why go on TV and over-share?
Those who don't trust you—who sighed in relief
at his crude grab-and-pull and your brief squeal—
may be foolish enough to think blond strands
are polygraph results, proof hard as steel
of your integrity. Still, why pander?
For years, draped on a white foam head, I've heard
my shop owner tell first-time buyers when
someone says their hair looks nice, not to blurt
It's fake. She adds, *Assume they don't know. Grin.*
In the case someone asks *Is that a wig?*
she gives permission to punch the rude pig.

Scrunchie to Hillary

Looped around your ponytail,
I traveled the world looking
past your ear, over your shoulder.

Your standard Secretary greeting—
So nice to meet you—rang
like a well-worn bell, followed

by a handshake, cheek-kissing
or, my favorite, a bow; you dipped
and beyond lowered heads

I could see fiery red pagodas,
Taiwan's record-tall skyscraper,
banana-laden boats dotting deltas.

You visited 112 countries,
more than any other Secretary,
and a ponytail was practical—

quick, no stylist necessary.
Before every landing, you piled
your long hair into one hand

then scooped me up, stretched out
my elastic middle, threaded hair
through me, twisting until I was snug.

Back home, Americans mocked
my casual white cotton, just as
they've mocked you forever.

Come, let's return to Perth—
its gusty wind made you laugh
and reach back to press me closer.

Butterfly Clip to Hillary

*Her less-than-perfect hair was not the issue; it was that she adorned
it with a silver butterfly clip—an accessory most commonly worn by
middle- and high-school girls.*
—Raquel Laneri, *Forbes*

The sun floats high
    over Manhattan traffic—
        if only your hair,
            which you've grown out
            in your new role
        as Secretary of State,
    could float
as far away;
shoulder-length strands
    slip from behind your ears
        and droop over your eyes
            as you skim world news.
            Here, try this,
        your assistant says
    and pulls me from her purse
where yesterday
her daughter
    accidentally
        dropped me
            while borrowing lip gloss.
            But the bad press
        I got for headbands
  and scrunchies…
you mutter and frown, rotating
me in your fingers
    like a rotisserie chicken.
        We've arrived,
            your driver says
            and pulls to the curb
        of the United Nations
    assembly building.

Quickly, you slide
your hands into the top
      and sides of your hair,
          gathering all but
              long pieces in back,
              then grip the half-
        portion of hair
    high and center
as your assistant
helps you open me—
      pinching my unfurled,
        spring-loaded
           wings together
           until they're
        back to back
    and my ten tiny prongs
unclasp and expand.
You nestle me in
    and around
        the separated hair,
           pat your liberated face,
           then you're out
        of the car onto a flag-
    edged sidewalk
into a lobby full of maroon
and oak furniture.
      You spot a friend and wave,
        his briefcase
           knocking yours
           as you hug.
        I need a gift
      for my girlfriend,
he says with an accent.
Who are your favorite
      clothing designers?
        The heavy doors

to the assembly hall
creak open
and men in suits
rush through them.
Would you ask
a man that question?
you say, barely smiling,
then take a step
toward the doors.
Once inside,
you find a seat
with other Americans
and a man on stage
booms *Welcome,*
world leaders.
What a title
you share with everyone
in this room,
such clout and power,
though I've seen
the embarrassing distractions
that come with
being a woman in your role.
My title, too,
promises more
than I actually am—
it's nice to look
like a butterfly
and perch on heads,
but what good is this
existence if I can't
fly, can't glide
so freely in my body
it's the only one I want?

Hairbrush to Hillary

Pay attention to your hair, because everyone else will.
—Hillary Clinton

Historians say my ancestor's
a paintbrush, velvety
horse hair dipped in a rainbow of oils.

These days I look more like a weapon—
long, steel handle and rigid bristles
capped with tiny, hard beads.

You've brushed your scalp raw
over the years; critics still sneer.
I wonder, what's your innermost hope
or fear? Here, paint it with me.

Hair Straightener to Hillary

I heat up to a whopping 450 degrees,
which is less than the number
of times I watched you manage a crisis
from your campaign makeup chair
as a stylist slithered me through your hair—
while she pressed my hot clamp
around your chin-length natural waves,
ironing the body out of each lock
from root to end then twisting me
to curl the tips around your face,
teaching your hair the lesson that waves
are only acceptable if man-made,
you applied similarly forceful
pressure to sudden catastrophes
brought to your attention
by cell phone alerts or huddled advisers—
in five minutes, you straightened out
online grumbling that you took too much
time off with pneumonia by tweeting
No Americans should be forced
to work while sick, flipping the script
to promote your health care reform,
then when graphs showed a dip
in your popularity among twenty-somethings
you shot up your index finger and said
Get that comedian on the phone
who interviews politicians between ferns,
and later the comedian called to say
he was running late to your filming
because of L.A. traffic, and while
your staff pored over online traffic reports
you proposed the comedian park his car
at a senator's house and your intern
with the moped retrieve him,
and every hairy situation
that came your way, you smoothed over

even if it meant not having an answer
and immediately seeking advice like when
WikiLeaks released yet another batch
of hacked emails and you rang staff
in swing states to ask what voters
wanted from you more, an explanation
of the emails or help paying their bills,
and in the last moments of your campaign,
when it was clear Trump would win,
your anger must have been immense
and yet you used that heat to even out
panic spreading across your country—
*Americans need to hear democracy
is safe,* you told your speechwriters early
that morning as a stylist clamped me on hair
she looped at your neck, and I never
saw you after that, though I heard
you escaped to the woods with your dogs,
two poodles with corkscrew fur, and I like
picturing your hair as frizzy as theirs,
the three of you roaming a winding path,
nothing too straight in your life now
and no problem to solve but when
to turn around and head home for dinner.

Comb to Hillary

*After the election, one of the things that helped me most...was going
back to the familiar experience of losing myself in books.*
—Hillary Clinton

Weeks after your loss, your bedroom
    reeked of bouquets
ready to throw out. Friends' calls
    dwindled

to text messages: *Hope you're OK.*
    So you plucked
Maya Angelou's *The Heart of a Woman*
    from your shelves,

sank onto your silk bedspread, and read
    for hours. Unexpectedly
Chelsea rang, and in a rush
    to mark your page

you snatched me from a stylist's pile
    of hair supplies,
forgotten in your bathroom
    post-campaign.

My fine, tiny teeth that once fluffed
    your wheat hair
nestled in the book's deep inner hinge.
    My long tail,

a skinny stick designed to slither through
    and section hair,
was as thin as the wispy pages,
    blending in.

I wasn't home but I was comfortable
    in smooth paper,

my topmost teeth peeking out
    for your return.

Like a skilled politician
    you found me work.
Now I dream of what else I can be:
    baton, letter opener, garden stake.

Hair Dye to Hillary

You're not going to see me turning white in the White House.
—Hillary Clinton

On election night, I wait in a box
with a row just like me hoping
to be bought, shipped, stored, uncapped.
I'm your shade, Light Honey Blond 8,
and according to packaging clerks
your victory is as good
as done. So I jiggle my gel, somersaulting
in my slim tube, as I anticipate
landing on a shelf
in America's most important home.
I picture the day I'll surf
your wavy hair, staining strands gold
and others bright porcelain,
depending how many minutes
your stylist lets me play before a rinse.

Now I've arrived at the house and shelf
I imagined, destined instead
for a twisty comb-over.
Maids whisper he only lets his wife
or daughter touch his hair, a blunt chop
straight across when, like ivy, strands creep
down his back collar.
Judging by his single-hue
butterscotch pouf and gray roots,
his family will apply me sloppily.
My milky gel curdles when I think back
on election night, my blind confidence in you
from a dark box where not once
did I consider if I can move, I can speak
and if I can speak, I can urge people to vote.

Blow Dryer to Hillary

I'm red with an easy-grip handle, long barrel
like a dolphin's nose, and cool-shot button that returns

your wispy hair to room temperature once it's dry.
A shot of cold reduces frizz, your stylist chirps,

and though she's right, the Kremlin only added that button
so I'd roar a minute longer.

Every day for seven-and-a-half minutes, I dart around your head
hoping horrid news breaks over radio,

text message dings, police sirens—anything detectable by sound.
I drowned out your staff's gasps the evening Bernie took Michigan,

boomed over *boos*
when Trump mocked your pneumonia.

When I impede your hearing, you're a fire truck arriving as the last
floor beam smolders;

when Comey re-opened your email investigation, a top adviser
tapped your shoulder, your stylist clicked me off,

and you were rushed away to make a statement,
shock like a tongue depressor

stilling your mouth.
The Kremlin won't stop at tampering with your ears;

in your stylist's hair and makeup bag is an arsenal altogether new
to American presidential politics—my comrade Eyeliner

made you miss Cruz dropping out on live TV.
My comrade Nail Polish ensured your fingernails weren't yet dry

seconds before Kaine
debated Pence. Your text message, sent too late, read *Hit hard.*

Hair Mousse to Hillary

On March's first warm day
you glided into a local salon.
The hairdresser, a friend, had cleared
the room, placing lit candles
on empty styling stations and piping
soft jazz through the speakers.
You hugged her and she asked
how you'd been. You described a fog
that engulfed you the second
your concession speech ended,
a fog that dulled green sugar
you and your granddaughter
sprinkled onto Christmas cookies,
that hovered above the New Year's ball
making its height look trivial,
the night sky a low ceiling,
a thick, numbing fog you thought
might entomb you until recently,
inexplicably, it'd begun to thin.
Wine tastes good again, you said.
You'd memorized a poem
about how time heals, and agreed
to speak to women in D.C. the following week.
The hairdresser squeezed your hand
and led you to her barber chair.
Bangs? she asked and you furrowed
your brows for a long minute, then nodded.
She combed and parted your hair
and with her fingers pantomimed
snipping three inches, then whisked
you to a sink and helped you
lean back. *You like the scent of roses?*
she asked and you said *Of course*
and she pulled a tube of rose shampoo
from a top shelf. *Can I razor
the ends of your hair for an edgy look?*
she asked as you returned to her chair.

You smiled, humming to Basie.
Your pale hair coated the floor
like snow. Before a blow-dry
and style, she presented a plate
of toasted almond-mocha truffles.
You each took one, recalling
the day you met in a bakery
two doors down. *Mousse okay?*
she asked and you grinned
and said *Yes, but just one bite,*
and there I was, a skinny, purple can
in the hairdresser's hand,
and she giggled and lifted me high
for you to see, then you giggled
and you both laughed hard, harder,
gasping, tears sliding down your faces.
It's the only time someone's
confused me for something,
and though I like my satiny
white, freesia-scented foam
it was exciting to imagine myself
as a bowl of decadent chocolate fluff
just as that day, you straddled two
selves, presidential hopeful
and everything that lies beyond—

Acknowledgments

I gratefully acknowledge the editors of the following journals or anthologies in which these poems first appeared.

The Cimarron Review: "False Eyelashes to Hillary" and "Nail Polish to Hillary"

The Missouri Review: "Brow Pencil to Hillary"

Nasty Women Poets: An Unapologetic Anthology of Subversive Verse: "Lipstick to Hillary"

Nebraska Quarterly: "Foundation to Hillary," "Powder to Hillary," and "Tweezers to Hillary"

Prairie Schooner: "Lip Liner to Hillary"

The Punch Magazine (World Poetry Portfolio): "Brow Brush to Hillary," "Butterfly Clip to Hillary," "Eye Shadow to Hillary," "Lip Gloss to Hillary," "Mascara to Hillary," "Retexturizing Cream to Hillary," "Scrunchie to Hillary" and "White Eyeliner to Hillary"

Notes (What's Not Made Up)

The speaking event I refer to in "Contact Lens to Hillary" is a commencement speech that Secretary Clinton gave at the all-women's Wellesley College on May 26, 2017. She was the commencement speaker at that college twice before, in 1969 (the year she graduated from Wellesley) and 1992.

The epigraphs for both "Brow Pencil to Hillary" and "Lip Gloss to Hillary" are from Clinton's speech in which she conceded the 2016 presidential election to Donald Trump. The speech took place on Nov. 9, 2016. In "Lip Gloss to Hillary," one quote is based off of Al Gore's speech conceding the 2004 presidential election to George W. Bush, in which he said, "Some have asked whether I have any regrets. And I do have one regret—that I didn't get the chance to stay and fight for the American people over the next four years…" I also quote from John McCain's speech conceding the 2008 presidential election to Barack Obama, in which he said, "And though we fell short, the failure is mine, not yours."

The epigraph for "Eyeliner to Hillary" is from remarks that Donald Trump made at a campaign rally in Wilmington, North Carolina, on Aug. 9, 2016.

In "Mascara to Hillary," my source for the early Egyptian and waterproof mascara formulas was the *Mental Floss* article "10 Facts About Mascara (to Help You Lash Out)" by Sarah Grossbart from Sept. 29, 2015. My source for the Roman mascara formula was the *My Beauty Matches* article "The Shocking History of Mascara" by Ivory Bella from April 9, 2015. The most comprehensive information about Lash Lure, the eyelash dye that blinded more than a dozen women, can be found at cosmeticsandskin.com, which quotes a 1933 *Time* article in which First Lady Eleanor Roosevelt responded to photographs of women affected by Lash Lure, saying, "I cannot bear to look at them."

The epigraph for "Brow Gel to Hillary" is from the National Bureau of Economic Research Working Paper Series "Why Don't Women Patent?" by Jennifer Hunt, Jean-Philippe Garant, Hannah Herman, and David J. Munroe from March 2012.

In "Eye Shadow to Hillary," the symposium I refer to is a Black Women's Agenda Symposium Workshop that took place in Washington, D.C., on Sept. 16, 2016, at which Clinton gave a campaign speech about policy ideas to meet African-American women's needs.

The speaking event I refer to in "False Eyelashes to Hillary" was a Children's Defense Fund gala in Washington, D.C., on Nov. 17, 2016—Clinton's first public appearance since her concession speech eight days before. News coverage of her Nov. 17 speech included *Glamour*'s headline "People are Loving that Hillary Clinton Went Make-up Free for Her First Post-Election Speech" and *The Telegraph*'s headline "Hillary Clinton laid bare: what her make-up free face might be telling us." The epigraph for this poem is from "Calon Lân," a Welsh song written in the 1890s by Daniel James.

The epigraph for "Foundation to Hillary" is from an interview with Jon Stewart by David Axelrod for his podcast *The Axe Files*. The interview took place on May 9, 2016.

The epigraph for "Face Primer to Hillary" is from Susan Bordo's 2017 book *The Destruction of Hillary Clinton* (Melville Press). In the sixth and seventh stanzas, I refer to Clinton's work in 1970 for Senator Walter Mondale's Subcommittee on Migratory Labor, interviewing migrant workers and their families; her work for Marian Wright Edelman in 1972 in Dothan, Alabama, where she posed as a mother looking for a school for her son while investigating whether or not a private school that had been granted tax-exempt status was discriminating because of race; and her work in 1973 in New Bedford, Massachusetts, for Edelman's Children's Defense Fund, knocking on doors to ask if differently-abled children lived there and were denied the opportunity to go to school.

The epigraph for "Retexturizing Cream to Hillary" is from a *Los Angeles Times* article, "The face of power," from Jan. 20, 2008. In the article, makeup artist Kriss Soterion said about Clinton's "dewy" face at a 2008 Democratic Party presidential debate, "I must have gotten a thousand e-mails about that afterward. Everyone wanted to know how I did it, what products I used."

The epigraph for "Blush to Hillary" is from a *Psychology Today* article, "5 Research-Backed Reasons We Wear Makeup," from Feb. 6, 2015.

The epigraph for "Blotting Paper to Hillary" is from an interview with Clinton by Tracy Clayton and Heben Nigatu for their BuzzFeed podcast *Another Round*. In the interview, which took place on Oct. 11, 2015, Clinton states that she is a robot, which, like the epigraph, is a joke.

The epigraph for "Chapstick to Hillary" is from remarks that Paul Gibson, president of the Sheet Metal Workers' Union, made at a campaign rally for Clinton on May 7, 2008. Clinton followed Gibson's remarks by saying, "I do think I have fortitude. Women can have it as well as men!"

In "Lip Liner to Hillary," the rumors I refer to originate from an anonymous email sent to the online magazine *Wonkette* from someone in Wasilla, Alaska. The email read, "Sarah's sister-in-law owns a beauty parlor in Wasilla…apparently Sarah's lip liner is tattooed on."

The epigraph for "Headband to Hillary" is from a *USA Today* article from 1992 titled "Hillary's hair bands: Zippy or just Dippy?"

The epigraph for "Wig to Hillary" is from an interview with Donald Trump by Mark Levin for Levin's radio show. The interview took place on Nov. 11, 2015. I also refer to an appearance that Clinton made on *The Tonight Show* with Jimmy Fallon on Sept. 17, 2015, during which she let Fallon pull her hair.

In "Scrunchie to Hillary," the public mockery of Clinton's scrunchie is documented in *The Huffington Post's* article "Hillary Clinton's Staff Wants to 'Ban' Her Scrunchies (Photos, Poll)" from April 6, 2012, as well as *The Daily Mail's* article "Scrunchie fan Hillary Clinton replaces outdated accessory with bejewelled hair tie (but is it actually any better?)" from Oct. 12, 2012.

The epigraph for "Butterfly Clip to Hillary" is from a *Forbes* article by Raquel Laneri, "Appearances Do Matter: Hillary Clinton's Hair Clip Controversy," from Sept. 24, 2010. The conversation in the poem between Clinton and a male politician is based off of a real incident that occurred in Bishkek, Kyrgyzstan, on Dec. 2, 2010. When the moderator of a town hall asked her, "Which designers do you prefer?" Clinton replied, "What, designers of clothes?" When the moderator answered, "Yes," she said, "Would you ever ask a man that question?"

The epigraph for "Hairbrush to Hillary" is from a commencement speech that Clinton gave at Yale University in May 2001. The connection in the poem between hairbrushes and paintbrushes came from a beauty stylist's blog, *Brigitte's Brushes*, where the blogger wrote, "One theory is that the paintbrush used for millions of years was slowly transformed into a hair-brush."

In "Hair Straightener to Hillary," the comedy show I refer to is *Between Two Ferns* with Zach Galifianakis; the episode starring Clinton aired on YouTube on Sept. 22, 2016. Clinton's statement in the poem that "Americans need to hear democracy is safe" is based off of details from the *New York* article "Hillary Clinton is Furious. And Resigned. And Funny. And Worried." from May 26, 2017. In the article, speechwriters Megan Rooney and Dan Schwerin describe Clinton telling them in the early morning of Nov. 9 that her concession speech should focus "on the protection of democratic norms." The rumors I refer to of Clinton escaping to the woods originate from a personal photo that Margot Gerster posted to Facebook on Nov. 10, 2016. Gerster and her daughter had been hiking in the woods near Chappaqua, New York, when they randomly encountered Clinton and Bill Clinton (who live nearby) walking their dogs, and Gerster asked if she could take a photo with Clinton.

The epigraph for "Comb to Hillary" is from a speech that Clinton gave at the American Library Association conference in Chicago, Illinois, on June 25, 2017. My reference to Maya Angelou's book *The Heart of a Woman* was inspired by Clinton's comment at the conference, "I re-read old favorites like Henri Nouwen's *The Return of the Prodigal Son,* the poetry of Maya Angelou and Mary Oliver."

The epigraph for "Hair Dye to Hillary" is from remarks that Clinton made at a campaign rally in South Carolina on May 27, 2015.

In "Mousse to Hillary," the hairstylist I refer to is Santa Nikkels, who owns Santa's Hair Salon in Chappaqua, New York, where Clinton resides.

Photo by Josh Fiedler

Marianne Kunkel is the author of *The Laughing Game* (Finishing Line Press) and holds a MFA in poetry from the University of Florida and a Ph.D. in English from the University of Nebraska-Lincoln. She is an assistant professor of creative writing and publishing at Missouri Western State University, director of the university's creative writing program, and editor-in-chief of *The Mochila Review.*

CPSIA information can be obtained
at www.ICGtesting.com
Printed in the USA
FSHW01n0506021018
52528FS

9 781622 882106